Anchor

Anchor

a collection

ABBIE WIGGINS

ANCHOR

First paperback edition September 2021

Book cover design by Abbie Wiggins
Forewords by Wendy Mann and Jane Kirby

ISBN 9798475620038

@wordsbyabbie on Instagram

To Becky and Sara

Table of Contents

Forewords

Abbie has such a gift when it comes to words. As I read through her book for the first time, I found myself feeling a whole range of emotions. I felt seen and known, I felt affirmed and comforted, and I felt hope rising in my heart. This is a book to take your time over. Don't rush through each poem. Instead, sit with the words and let the truth really impact your heart and mind. In a world where so much is changing all the time, this book is full of inspiration and hope to anchor your soul.

I am so proud of Abbie for the many hours she has given to producing this book. I know that the words within it will have a deep and profound effect on many people's lives. I pray you will enjoy the journey.

Wendy Mann
wendymannequip.com
Author of Naturally Supernatural and Leading as Sons and Daughters

I'm not sure if this is a term or not, but somehow it seems to sum up what this book is full of and it's *creative wisdom*. The words Abbie chooses and the way she uses them is beautiful. This is the sort of book that you want to keep by the side of your bed to read a page a night or when you wake up in the morning. Anchor really will take you to somewhere deeper and you'll really be richer for reading it.

Jane Kirby
rebelheartsrebelgirls.com
Founder of Rebel Hearts Rebel Girls and editor of Truth Magazine

Acknowledgements

Thank you for choosing to pick up this book. Wherever you are, I hope that you find peace and light in these pages. I'm glad you're here and I'm thankful for you.

Mum, dad, Becky and Sara. You are a constant source of laugher and adventure. Team Wiggins! I love you guys.

Hannah, your friendship is one I know I can always count on. You're my person.

Wendy, your encouragement, love, wisdom and friendship are a gift. I love our walks and deep chats. You teach me how to live more like Jesus.

Sarah, you're full of joy. Thank you for encouraging me to keep going after my dreams. You inspire me.

Sally, you saw me and invested in me. I wouldn't be where I am today without your wisdom and kindness.

Kiah, thank you for all of your editing wisdom. You poured your heart into helping me make this collection into what is it today.

Thank you Anna, Kate, Tim, Emma, Lizzie, Ben and Natalia. Your friendship means the world to me.

Preface

When I was writing this collection, the word 'anchor' kept coming into my mind. An anchor holds a boat steady, keeps it in place, stops it from drifting away. What holds us steady when life gets hard? What are we anchored to? These are the questions I was thinking about as I put this book together. My heart is that these words will bring you hope and peace as you read them. Feel free to write, draw or doodle on the pages. This is a safe space, an anchor.

abbie

Sit down,
take the time to let yourself feel
what you need to feel.
Let it all out
and breathe.

BREATHE

I kept my eyes closed and called it safety,
but hiding isn't freedom
and I wanted to be free.

So I let the walls come down
and the light came in
to shine where the shadows had been.

I stared at the ground,
shame controlling my gaze.
Then I felt warm hands
against my tear streaked face.

As you lifted my head,
my eyes were met with love
like I'd never felt before
and I knew I was free.

To stop means to listen
to thoughts long-buried in
constant distraction.

When I'm forced to be still
I fight the silence,
there's an internal war.

But day by day,
peace replaces heaviness
as I begin to let go of
what was never mine to carry.

You feel like it's your responsibility
to fix everything,
to keep the peace,
to carry on,
to be okay all the time,
to be someone other people can lean on.

You are important too.

In the middle of the storm,
lead me to quiet spaces
where I don't just catch my breath,
but allow the air to fill my lungs.

I know what it's like to
live in a fog, waiting for it to lift.
Clouded thoughts and numbed emotions
should never be taken lightly.

I want you to remember that
the fog won't last forever, it will lift.

Joy and hope are possible because
this season is not your whole story.

Unravel the ideas in your mind about
who you think you should be.

The world needs the real you.

You are precious to me.

I will never ask you to be
anyone other than who you are.

You've believed the lie that
you're not enough,
but believe me when I say
you're worth everything.

It's harder now
than it's ever been before.
You're tired,
I know.

It's okay to cry,
let yourself cry.
Don't rush through the pain,
let it all out.

I see you rising up in freedom.
I see you being made whole again.
I see you telling the story
of how you made it through this storm.

I looked in the mirror yesterday
and something was different,
where pain had been, was hope.

I don't know how, but over time,
more and more light had broken through
and I knew I had been restored.

The pieces of who I thought I needed to be
fade away as I begin to realise that
who I am is already enough.
Now, I want to feel things deeply again.

NEVER ALONE

I know you're afraid of
what comes next,
but I want you to know
that whatever it is
I'll be right by your side.

When you feel like you're alone
remember that I am in the boat with you.
I will never abandon you.

I'll cry with you
along your darkest roads
and laugh with you
on the mountain tops.

I'll pick up the pieces of your heart
and hold them gently in my hands,
I'll put them back together
and love you with all I am.

The battle you're fighting
won't last forever.
There is hope,
a future
beyond this.

You can talk to me
when your heart is heavy.
You can come to me
when your thoughts are loud.
Your heart is safe here.
You are safe here.

You will be okay,
but that doesn't mean
you have to face things
on your own.

If you're not okay,
tell me you're not okay.
I want to see the real you,
not the version you think I want to see.

When you feel sad,
you can come to me.
I'll listen.
I'll never turn you away.
I hear you, even when you
don't have the words to say.

I am here.
I always have been.
I always will be.

GROWTH

Today, when I stood there
in front of the mirror again,
something was different.
Slowly, without even realising,
I had come to know myself.

Don't stay on the shore.
It might be where you land,
but it's not where you stay.

I want you to know that
stepping away from
something harmful
is okay.
It's not abandoning
or giving up,
it's knowing how much
you're worth.

It's okay if you don't know
what's going to happen next,
don't think so much about the future
that you forget to live now.

Don't let the
voice of doubt
stop you from
being who you are,
let the voice of love
remind you of
who you are.

Don't believe the lie that says,
"You should be okay by now."
You are worth a heart set free.

Be as kind,
as patient
and as gentle
with yourself
as you are
with others.

Find a place
where you can breathe,
a place where
you can be yourself.

Some of the best advice I've ever been given is to find out both w
brings you peace and what takes it away.

To the beaten down hearts
and burned out minds,
this is not your forever.

COURAGE

Your steps of courage are powerful,
they will lead you to places
where you'll dance on waves
you used to run from.

It's time to stop hiding,
come into the light, be seen.
Stand up and brush off the dust
that was never meant to settle on you.

Don't let fear determine
the path you follow.
Let courage take
you by the hand.
There is so much
more for you.

If love is a shield
and my armour is hope,
there will be peace
in this storm.

Don't discount yourself.
You were created to do things
beyond what you can imagine right now.

I'm learning that
letting out the tears
is brave.

Over and over
I remind myself that
fear does not control me.

ANCHOR

You've come all this way
and now,
it's time to step out.

Don't worry,
I'll be here
the whole time.

BE THE LIGHT

I told the darkness about light
and it trembled with fear.

Sometimes,
the best thing you can do for
someone who's struggling is listen, really listen.
Don't rush on, or brush their words aside.
Listen.
Make space for them to be heard.

Someone once told me a story of a time when they almost decided to give up. I asked what it was that stopped them.

"It was the way a stranger smiled at me, their eyes full of joy like I'd never seen before. I knew that what they had would be possible for me one day too."

Quiet kindness is
loud in the hearts of
those that receive it.

I hope you know
how brightly you shine.
The light inside you
will be what brings life into the
unreached shadows of people's hearts.

The way your heart radiates love
leads everyone around you
back to hope.

I'm reminded again of
how important it is to be kind,
to throw away any prejudices
and stand with people
in their storms.

Be someone who
makes everyone feel
seen and loved.

Be someone who
lets everyone know
that they belong.

Decide to only speak lovingly
about yourself and others.

Be the one who
defiantly refuses to be
anything other than kind.

What if, instead of breaking, we built?

Set on fire with hope,
we will change the world with
outrageous love
that sends darkness running
and heals broken hearts.

I was a boat without an anchor,
every wave threatening to steal my safety.
Then love rescued me, held me steady
and I knew no wave could drown me again.

THE END

NOTES

NOTES

NOTES

ABOUT THE AUTHOR

Abbie Wiggins was born in 1996 near Cardiff, Wales. She grew up in Holland and France before moving back to the UK with her family in 2015. In 2019, she received a BA (Hons) in English Literature from the University of Brighton. Abbie started posting her writing on Instagram in 2018 with the aim to spread hope through social media.

Printed in Great Britain
by Amazon